Lemonade and Silver Linings

Coming Out On Top When Things Go Wrong

An Ignite and Inspire Series Book

Joy

MJP Publishing LLC

To Ivory. I admire you! Your constant effort at growing yourself, living what you teach, and serving others is a head shaking, heartwarming inspiration! Thank you for being in my life. I love you, sister.

To Benjamin Hardy, PhD. You don't know me (yet); however, your work has impacted me since I first encountered your blog in 2015. It has been a true joy watching you blossom and your family grow! I am ever grateful for your content, and more importantly for your integrity and genuineness.

Table of Contents

Introduction

**Getting knocked down in life is a given...
getting up and moving forward is a choice ~
Zig Ziglar**

Lemonade and Silver Linings is intended to help you handle hurt, offense, setbacks, disasters, injustice, unfairness, disappointment, you know – life. Be it big or small, intense grief or something mildly perturbing, or anything in between, what are you going to do with it? *And*, will you like yourself on the other side of it?

Napoleon Hill said, "If life hands you a lemon, don't complain, but instead make lemonade to sell to those who are thirsty from complaining". My rendition: When bad things happen, turn it for good. There is nothing good in bad, sad, depressed, or disappointment. There's *nothing* there for you; so why stay?

"Oh, Joy, you don't know what I've been

through". Well, you don't know what I've been through either and frankly, it shocks people when they hear some of my stories because I don't look or act like someone that has experienced every kind of abuse, been homeless, hungry, and abandoned multiple times. That's because I have done what I teach in this book and have come out stronger and better each time.

Be encouraged. Even if we don't share the same past you can still benefit from this book because let's face it, yuck happens. Be assured, you *can* live a happy and fulfilling life, now. Today. You don't have to wait to have peace, rest, joy and happiness in the sweet by and by. And this book is going to give you the tools to make that happen in your own life.

Here is your caution. If you think that you will skim these pages and then bibbity bobbity boo, all, *insert your own bad word here*, is gone, you will be intensely disappointed. There is effort on your part and, as with anything new, it will take mind renewal and practice. The up side is that the more you employ your newfound understanding, the easier it will become and then one day you will realize that things that used to grate your final nerve simply... don't. You will find that things that would upend your day no longer impact you. And, when life throws a lemon at you, pelts you with many, or backs up with a dump truck load of them, you will be armed to overcome, making your lemonade and turning something good from it by seeing the silver lining. Because, there *always* is one.

There's a line in a song that says "you've gotta face the clouds to find the silver lining". Taking this perspective with you everywhere you go is essential to living a life of internal peace even when the world around you seems to be falling apart. *Don't put the book down.* I am not saying that you have to become fake and pretend things aren't happening. We are actually going to acknowledge the mess that just landed in your life, *then* put it in a perspective that *enables* you to overcome... to grow... to not let it define you. Did you read that? Instead of said pile determining your life trajectory, you are *empowered* to move past it. *You* decide what defines you, not the lemons.

I get it, you may be in searing emotional pain right now. Your mind may be screaming. You may have not slept much in weeks because of this awfulness. Or, you may just be tired of a lemon pelting or thundercloud overhead impacting you so deeply. You want to be able to shake it off, maintain your dignity and self-respect, and come out a better version of you. *It is possible.* I am living proof of it. Time and again. And so can you.

Does this mean that I am perfect and have no opportunities to practice this anymore? (Did you just hear me laugh?) Heck no. While our lemons and thunderclouds are different, the process is the same. My point is that the depth of the suffering isn't applicable in the process. I know that sounds harsh. Again, be encouraged, you'll see what I mean as we progress.

Lastly, this book is not an end all. There is no way for me to touch on each possible scenario and list every type of help out there. What this book contains are sure, founded, tried and true methods to get the ball rolling, your feet under you, peace in your heart, hope in your days, and a sense of confidence and purpose to propel you forward. You read that correctly. You will *strengthen* and *grow* in this process! Instead of being the same or worse, you will be better! Part of your continued growth is to seek out other modalities that may benefit your specific need. I will touch on that in Chapter 6 and have provided a *Resources by Chapter* section on my website as well as a *Discussion Group and Community* to support you. (See the end of Chapter 7 for more information.)

What to Expect

Here's what you will find in this book: A loving but in your face reality of how to handle lemons, the real meaning and purpose behind silver linings, how to maintain peace through the mess, and how to continue growing once you are on the other side. This is rinse and repeat regardless of the offense type or size. The action steps may be different with each situation, but the process is the same. This is what I used when my (first) husband and son went camping and never returned home (huge!), when I found out that one of my dearest friends was betraying me (awful), when I lost my job and none of my coworkers ever checked on me (hurtful), all the way to the bozo that felt it necessary to cut me off while changing lanes almost causing me to crash (not cool, dude). Same process, different action steps.

Your Part

What's your part in all of this? Continue reading beyond this introduction, revisit sections of the book as needed, answer the questions at the end of each chapter honestly, and make use of the free resources and community set up to support you. Don't just skim through this looking for a magic bullet. I promise you, there aren't any. However, you *can* read this book looking for what you can apply today to start changing your life *right now*, to reduce the pain *right now*, to stop the jumbled thoughts *right now*, to regain a foothold and stop the spiraling *right now*. Those are big promises, yet I can say it with confidence because I have lived these many times over. Life happens to all of us, not just you. If this process can help me to be a happy, life enjoying, motivated, excited person, and has helped many others, then it can help you.

So, grab a notebook and prepare to notate your journey and also use it to answer the questions at the end of each chapter, not in your head, in writing. Believe me, you will be glad that you did. Soon you will be able to see the progress. It's motivating to look back and see that what was a seemingly endless set of days and nothingness was really movement. It's thrilling! But you won't experience it if you don't do what's asked of you and if you don't start now. So, let's do that. Let's get started. *Right now.*

Chapter 1
Lemons: The Negative Impactor

I'm proud of you for turning the page! If you don't have pen or pencil and something to write on, go get that now. This is a hands-on process. You may want to make notes, write down ideas as they come to you, or even put the book down and just write your thoughts or feelings. This notebook is going to serve you very well as you actively engage with what you are learning here. It will also serve you in a few weeks, months, and years when you look back and see how far you have come. You have to just trust me on this. Please take this portion seriously. Do you have your paper and pen? Alright, let's get into it!

So, what are lemons? They are the things that came in and negatively impacted your lunch break, career, whole day, movie watching experience, drive to the store, relationship, evening, weekend, or even life as you know it, such as: rudeness, hurt, offenses, death, setbacks, disasters, injustice, lying, abandonment, unfairness, loss, disrespect, and disappointment.

How do you know it was a lemon? Was it negative? Then it was a lemon. Size does not matter. It was the opposite of good, therefore, it is a lemon. Let's say someone decides to leave the back of the line to 'hang out' with their friends who are also in line, *in front of you.* One person may genuinely not be moved by that, another may be annoyed but blow it off and others, even now, have felt their blood pressure leap. Why? Because it's rude, disrespectful, selfish, and discourteous. Plain and simple. And it's not fair!

No, it's not. It's not fair when your spouse takes off with someone else, when you twist your ankle the night before the big race you've trained months for, when someone steals your lunch from the refrigerator at work, when you are thrown under the bus/lied about, when you are slighted, ghosted, or blown off, when your child dies, when it is *your* tire that rolls over the nail and goes flat, when a house guest breaks a favorite item, when the doctor gives you a bad report, when your best friend moves away, when your cell phone got wet and died, when you slipped and dinner is now all over the floor, when when when... dang lemons. As you see, they are both tiny and huge, and they can negatively impact.

Big or small, intense or not so much, where we want to get is to not let it steal our inner peace *and* to maintain our dignity and self-respect through it. *Keep reading.* I know that some of you read that last statement and rolled your eyes moaning, "here we go again with the peace stuff". First of all, I get that you are in pain, but stop with the attitude. I am trying to help. So, put your teachable hat on, hear what I have to say (I purposefully made this a short read), apply it, *then* judge. I believe that you will be pleasantly surprised. As we progress you will learn to not see the depth or breadth of the issue, just the path out. Not only that, but you will come to the point where things really just don't bother you. I don't mean you pushing it down or refusing to give voice to it, but it *genuinely doesn't affect you.* Ahhhhh – nice breath of fresh air right there! Can you *imagine* such a life? That's not rhetorical. Go ahead, give it a thought. Close your eyes, breathe for a moment, and imagine not being crazy over the fact that that person cut in line.

[This is where you close your eyes and imagine.
Yeah, I was serious.]

Did you feel more in control? Did you feel a bit more dignified? Did you overall feel better about yourself not giving in to frustration or even rage? If not, it's ok; you'll get there.

The Decision Point

Let's start with the decision point. Viktor Frankl said, "Between stimulus and response there is a space. In that space is our power to choose our response. In our response lies our growth and freedom". Basically, there is a moment of time where we *know* it's decision time. The more aware you become of it, the faster you will recognize it, the fewer blunders you will make and the more dignity you retain and the more respect you gain for yourself and with others. The little voice is sometimes hard to hear, so let's start with the big, loud voice. That voice is asking you to decide now, are you going to lay down and die or are you going to thrive? You are standing there, right now, foreclosure papers in hand. Now what? You gonna crawl under the bed and call all of your friends frantically telling them how awful your life is and poor me and why me and and and...? You *do* have the option of finding a different path. Sure, it may still end in foreclosure, but what state are *you* in during and after the process?

Anxiety, depression, fear, and grief are real, are tangible, and are killing you. Keep in mind that emotions are fleeting, but actions impact and produce movement. The loud voice is saying that you are at a crossroads. You don't know what either road looks like, but one has a definite bad and ugly ending and the other one has at least a chance of a brighter outcome. Once you have picked the brighter course, then you move on to the finer details of seeing the path, overcoming, and then maintaining your victory, ultimately being a story to tell to encourage others and even yourself should trying times arise again.

The decision point is something that you will come back to time and again and as already mentioned, the better you get at detecting it, the more and faster you will see it. This contributes to you having more control over your days, thus your future, and over your emotions and mental state, thus your quality of life. You will start to see growth in many areas and genuinely feel better about yourself, *even* with the sky falling all around you. *Yes*, you can get to that place of peace and rest right in the middle of a storm. The next few chapters have examples of what decision points look like in real life to give you some visuals. For now, let's recap what we have learned.

Recap

So far we know what a lemon is, that regardless of the intensity, it doesn't have to impact you the same as it always has, that you do have control over the impact it has on you, that you have a decision point and it starts with are you taking the dead end or the hopeful road, and that the more you employ just these few things the stronger and happier you will be and become. As you continue reading, you will have more understanding how to do and experience this. For now, remember that all of it starts with your very next decision point. Go ahead, look for it, big or small, look for the decision point, then grin when you see it. You are well on your way!!

Back to the matter at hand: the bottom line is, the lemons have pelted, maybe even the dump truck scenario has hit. That sucks. There is no pleasantry about a tornado ripping apart a home, a car catching fire, your best friend dying, and so on. Nope. So, let's do this. Let's face this head on. We aren't going to turn a blind eye to it and hold our breath wishing it would all go away. No matter *how much* we want that person back, wish we had followed that inner voice that told us to turn left and not right, and so on, what's done is done. We are here. We are now. Remember the line in the song "you gotta face the clouds to find the silver lining".

Ok, then let's find the silver lining and get outta here!

Questions and Action Steps
Chapter One

Answering these questions will help you start to realize the power that you already possess, which leads to hope and encouragement.

- Did you imagine your reaction to the person cutting in line? If you didn't go ahead and do it now. It just takes 60 seconds. Try to imagine yourself one level less upset than you normally would be.

- Whether you did it while reading or just now, what are the positive things you are seeing and feeling about yourself? If you still feel anything less than calm or unmoved, it's ok, you'll get there. I encourage you to at least try. Every so often try to see it one level better and then the next. A smile will spread across your face the first time that you are able to do it and there will be a little victory dance going on inside. Those of you that were able to see yourself taking it up a level, if you wanna boogie right now just a lil bit, go for it! I am all about celebrating victories!

- How do you think that recognizing the decision points in your life will positively impact you?

- The dead end or the brighter option, either road will not be a cake walk. Do you see the benefit of choosing one over the other?

- Share your answers, questions, and thoughts in the Discussion Group. Let's support and encourage each other! You can also visit the resources for this chapter on my website.

Chapter 2
Silver Linings: They are in Your Perspective

General George Patton stated, "Success is how you bounce on the bottom". Well, here you are, smelling like lemons. I guess this is your chance to bounce, and you might as well bounce high and change the view. That's what a silver lining is, changing your view of the situation. It's what makes the lemon scenario less painful, *and* is the gateway to healing and better days. It is your path out of the muck, confusion, and stress. In plain language, these silver linings are found in your perspective. It's a shift in your viewpoint and is extraordinarily powerful! Yet it is so simple that a child can do it. And most do until adults teach them otherwise. You should watch little ones some time in their innocence and ability to see the brighter side, then join them.

In the 1960 Disney movie *Pollyanna*, the orphan girl is far too happy considering where she came from and her current situation, yet she always is. It's because of her perspective. "Instead of looking at the bad, let's find something to be glad about," she says. Ok, so that is a bit simplistic, but the idea is quite valid. Why *not* look for the good as you stand there dripping in lemon juice? Do you have a better solution? How's that worked out for you in the past? Thought so. Let's keep going.

Perspective makes all the difference because you are 1) acknowledging it. There is no freedom or growth in sticking your fingers in your ears, eyes closed chanting la-la-la-la or burying your head in the sand, alcohol, shopping, food, sex, TV shows, video games, or other things that *do not* make the situation go away. It just elongates and makes it worse, and in some cases, way worse; 2) then putting it in its *correct* place by what you think on.

There is no escaping the immediacy of an issue. You still have to face your angry client, pack up the house, bury your loved one, get the car fixed, change your coffee-soaked shirt, make the phone call, and clean up the spill. The silver lining, perspective, is what starts the turn of the situation from hell with *no* end to a light *at* the end. Make no mistake about it; you are going through it. The questions are 1) can it be less painful as you do and 2) can you be a better person on the other side of it? The answer to both is a resounding yes! Am I promising an effortless, journey? No. However, I know experientially how the same scenario played out this time doesn't gouge me like it did last time. How in the past, what would have laid me up for two months, this time it took only two hours. I'm telling you; *this is real*.

Perspective is the way that you see something. When you have a very narrow view of a situation, you are not seeing the bigger scenario which means you may also be missing your exit-this-awful-situation sign. So how do you see it? You must first start with the decision between am I going to see this as hope*less* or hope*ful*? That is the crossroads question. Once you decide that, then the path appears as the answers start to come. Steven Covey said, "I am not a product of my circumstances. I am a product of my decisions." That's right. *You* decide. But how? Mindset.

Mindset

Your mindset (a major component of your perspective) is comprised of everything you have read, seen, heard, and experienced in the entirety of your life. Whoa! That's big! True. *And you get to control it.* The science and depth of clearing out belief systems (what makes up your mindset) takes up the space of many large books. Getting to the root cause moves you along faster, but until you can dive into one of those books, this still works. Believe me, I know. For now, I am going to simplify it for you. Let's start by focusing on what you can control right now. As it relates to mindset, right now, you definitely have control over 1) what you think on 2) what you ingest through your eyes and ears and 3) what you say.

The Power Of What You Think On

My (second) husband and I had been separated only a few months on July 4 that year. We still spoke at times and even discussed counseling and reconciling. July 4 was a special day for us and as it approached, I just *knew* he was going to surprise me with a day full of adventure and activities, just like we had done in the past. As the date grew closer, I couldn't wait any longer and asked him about his July 4 plans. He was going to spend it with 'her'. I was utterly crushed and the reality of why we were no longer together settled deep into the marrow of my bones. I cried so hard that I could not breathe at times. Sitting on the floor, my sobbing continued and then something hit me. (The decision point – you are now aware and you now get to decide). I looked up to see the clock. Realizing that nearly four hours had passed since reading that text message, I decided that enough was enough. (I chose a path.) The tears seemed to stop almost immediately as I blew my nose. I took a shower and had a talk with myself. (Action steps toward that path.)

Fast forward a few days later. It is now July 4. Being a holiday, I was not at work but home, alone. My friends were all out of town and I was not up for being around a crowd of strangers. This was *our* day and he was spending it with *her*! I got up and went back to bed, got up and went back to bed, over and over, finally staying up and took a shower. I was never able to hide in sleep because my mind kept grinding over the thoughts of them. I imagined last July 4, but in every scenario instead of me, I saw her. She was in the kayak beside his, she was in the lawn chair next to his on the botanical gardens' lawn listening to the Symphony play, she is who he looked at lovingly, and whose hand he held. This continued through just staring at and not eating my lunch, going for a walk, and trying to take a nap (I really wanted relief from these thoughts!). It was nearly 3:00 pm when I realized (decision point) that I felt only worse and drained as the day went on and further realized it *was because I gave all of my energy to thinking about them.* I threw my shoes on and headed back out for another walk, this time my mind excited. I was on to something! By the end of my second trip around the block, I had stopped thinking about them and started thinking about *my* future. I felt energy come back and a lightheartedness begin to fill me. After all of those wasted hours, how did that happen so quickly?

Whatever you think on is what will be magnified; it becomes bigger and ultimately takes up your entire windshield. Sure, you may see bits and pieces of things along the sides, *but the conversations and plays you repeat in your head is what defines your view.* What you magnify is what 'is' and you get/live/experience what you 'see'. Did you notice how I was dying slowly as the day progressed, but with the flip of my thoughts, I started to come alive again? We will go deeper into this in the next chapter. For now, let's go over the basics.

[Here is where I am asking you to put the book down, for just a moment, close your eyes and breathe, just a few, head clearing breaths, then re-read that last paragraph. We are about to step into mind renewal. I know you want to stop the pain, move this forward, get out of this hell hole, or just adjust your thinking about crappy situations, but you cannot swallow this whole and think you'll digest it. Seriously, let's chew this so it becomes a part of you, a new way of thinking, and *then* we experience the changes. Go ahead and set the book down, breathe for a moment, re-read that last paragraph, then continue to the reset.]

The Reset Begins

How do you see your situation? Whatever it is, that is your perspective *based on your perception* of the situation. You view the situation to be one way so that is how it is for you. What if your perception/view of the situation was adjusted? Could you then see it differently? Seeing it differently so that you can have better results than the bleakness that is currently before you?

What life do you want? What defines you? Are you willing to see that there are other sides to this situation? That there could be a better outcome? That you could be a better version of yourself? The bottom line is that you can make excuses or you can make changes. Your choices today will land you somewhere. And if you do nothing, by default, you've chosen the hopeless route.

I want to be candid with you; this takes guts. This takes effort. Please also hear this: *it is SO worth it!* And I will also warn you now, it may not be pretty. Taking a higher or different road is not for the faint of heart. Before you resign to failure and put the book down, please, just finish this book. Again, it is intentionally short so that you can get through it quickly. **You have *so much* more inside of you than you think that you do!** I wouldn't have believed it about myself if I hadn't experienced it time and again. But it is true. It was and is for me and it can be for you.

Many years ago, I was so insecure that my wardrobe was made up mostly of plain t-shirts and jeans. I wanted to blend in, not be seen. As a matter of fact, I could be heard saying and most definitely thinking "I am the wall". No one really looks at walls. No one pays attention to a wall. They mindlessly go around it. *If I am quiet, no one will see me.* I thought that a lot too. And then, like I hadn't already had it pretty rough in my past, life backed up the biggest dump truck of lemons it could find right into my world. My family didn't come home from their camping trip. I went from a 20-year wife, best friend, business partner, 16-year mom, nurturer, home maker, and volunteer to single and alone. I went from an abundance of noise to silence that was deafening. I went from an assured future, purpose, and identity to a nothing, a nobody in 24 hours. Well, what was being the wall going to do for me then? I'm telling you; *YOU CAN DO THIS!*

I don't care how many times you have to put the book down and go for a walk or stand on the porch letting the sun warm you or take a shower or whatever. (I used to stand in the rain and eventually danced in it and even splashed in the mud – all more than once!) Just please, please, come back and pick this up. The person that you are 6 months from now, a year from now, will thank you for doing it, for making these hard choices. I give you my word, this *will* be worth it. Just watch. You'll see. Do what is asked of you, follow these steps, take this seriously, and notate your path in your notebook.

You are still here. *I'm so proud of you!* Let's keep going.

Questions and Action Steps
Chapter Two

Answering these questions will help you to adjust your perspective and start seeing silver linings, possibilities, paths, doors that you didn't even know where there. The more you magnify this more positive/hopeful viewpoint, the more opportunities and open windows you will experience. You will also notice that things inside of you are calming down a smidge, or a lot. Again, we celebrate every victory regardless of size.

- What life do you want? What defines you? These answers can be as simple or detailed as you want them to be. You will find that as you continue, your vision of the real you, the you that you want to be, will grow and become clearer.

- Imagine your life minus, over, or around this issue. Jot a few words or sentences of what life without this loss or pain or injustice looks like. You can have that, and even better. Maybe you just focus on how much more calm you are, that you didn't have to get blood pressure or anxiety medicine, that you no longer run to the refrigerator, your phone, or some other 'anesthetic', instead you feel bolder and confident.

- Even if you don't feel those now, can you see you being that? Can you see 3 months down the road? 6 months? 1 year? Can you see this one day being a fleeting thought/a faint memory/an encouraging story? Keep practicing so that it becomes clearer in your mind. Do it while you walk, shower, clean, cook, get ready for bed or the day, or instead of scrolling through social media.

- Write how your story ends. You can write, type, voice to text the story, like you are telling it to someone confidently, victoriously, "I remember, 3 months ago when...". Keep this before you. Read it, and even add to it as you go. It's *your* life. Go ahead and paint it the way that you want it to be.

- Share your goals with the Discussion Group. It's a great idea to let others in to root for and cheer you on. You may also find that there are people there who could use your words of encouragement and learn from your lessons. You can also look at the resources for this chapter on my website.

Chapter 3
Stop the Spinning

D r. Benjamin Hardy instructed, "Never be offended that your new circumstances require you to change... Rather than simply going where you need to go, be willing to become who you need to become." The fact is, you are in it. Right now, you are somewhere between 'I don't like how I react and want more self-control' and 'I am in a living hell, get me out!'.

The last chapter reminded that you are in control of what you think about, say, and consume through your eyes and ears. This and the next few chapters will go deeper into those, and applying that information will produce the mind renewal needed for change. That is how, as discussed earlier, you get to the place where things simply don't impact you like they used to. When big things that would have previously bowled you over make you only teeter just a bit, you know that you have strengthened. As you pursue a new mindset, you will start to see many benefits. Watch for them. Some come slowly (revisiting your notebook will help) and some will leap you to another place in life and mental clarity.

Controlling What You Think On

Taking control of what you allow to roll around or replay in your mind is a huge step toward mind renewal. A few things that you can expect as you take charge of what is allowed to hang out in your mind are: reduced or no anxiety, fear, and anger, thus blood pressure; your life will become increasingly less dramatic; you will have a more refreshed and/or dignified view of yourself; better sleep; fewer weird cravings; and as you can imagine, it protects your health. Your mind is *your* mind to be directed wherever *you* choose. Yes, you have a choice. Sit back for a moment while I tell you some stories.

The following story is attributed to different Native American tribes with general variations:

The Story of the Two Wolves

An old Cherokee is teaching his grandson about life: "A fight is going on inside me," he said to the boy. "It is a terrible fight and it is between two wolves. One is evil – he is anger, envy, sorrow, regret, greed, arrogance, self-pity, guilt, resentment, inferiority, lies, false pride, superiority, and ego." He continued, "The other is good – he is joy, peace, love, hope, serenity, humility, kindness, benevolence, empathy, generosity, truth, compassion, and faith. The same fight is going on inside you and inside every other person, too.

The grandson asked his grandfather: "Which wolf will win?"

The old Cherokee simply replied, "The one you feed."

Then there's the real-life story of Viktor Frankl who authored multiple books, holds 2 doctorates, is the creator of Logotherapy, a husband, father, and a concentration camp survivor. Hopefully you are aware of the atrocities of such a place so we'll fast forward to: he has lost his parents, siblings, pregnant wife, livelihood, home, and seemingly anything worth living for. Yet, he said this: "Everything can be taken from a man but one thing: the last of the human freedoms – to choose one's attitude in any given set of circumstances, to choose one's own way".

In both of these stories we see how real choice is. Choosing to redirect your mind may not be easy at first. If you are used to allowing it to wander down unhealthy roads, you have to practice reining it back in. If you are used to playing the same recording over and over again: "I'm not good enough", "If only", the argument last night, the incident at work, etc it's time to break that record! How?

In Chapter 1, you were introduced to the decision point. Hopefully by now you are starting to see it more and are taking advantage of it to increasingly gain control of your life. If not, start today.

When you realize (the decision point) that you are chewing on those thoughts, replaying the record, however you want to put it, that is when the power of choice kicks in. This is one of those hard things discussed earlier; you *have* to kick those thoughts out, utterly refuse to give them any more mental space. Change the channel. Don't let those thoughts magnify themselves! This can look an infinite set of ways, but it all comes down to the word 'stop'. You have to stop the spinning, the downward spiral egged on by the words and visuals staying forefront in your mind. As you can imagine, this may not be easy at first. However, as you practice, it becomes easier. You realize it faster and can stop it sooner so the situation has less of a chance to have a hold on you. Let's illustrate the 'stop'.

You've made it through the morning go go go, everyone is up, ready, fed and off to their respective places. Half of a cream cheese bagel in hand, you manage to open the car door, get your purse/briefcase/backpack, beverage container, and all of you into the car. Door closed. *Ahh... silence.* With a satisfyingly deep inhale and equally refreshing exhale you turn the key, set your radio station or audio book to play and put 'er in reverse. Backing slowly out of the driveway you put that wonderful bagel up to your lips when a jogger passes by your driveway. Startled, you overcompensate and slam instead of touch your breaks. This smushes the cream cheese up your nose which causes you to drop the bagel onto your slacks and now what? (decision point) There are a lot of physical scenarios we can play out. Do you change your clothes? Wipe the pants and hope for the best? So, let's go with you are in a hurry so the bagel goes into the trash can in your car (yes, I have a little trash can in my car), the glove box provides ample napkins to clean off your pants and out your nose, one look in the mirror to verify all is well visually, and you are off.

Your first very natural emotion is probably surprise. Let's be honest, you weren't expecting someone to show up running along the end of your driveway, you have a nostril filled with cream cheese, and have now adorned your pants with said cheese. What is going through your mind as you wipe, blow, clean, and clear?

- Dmit! – As you reach for the napkins
- Effing jogger! – As you wipe feverishly
- I *knew* today would suck! Things went way too well this morning.
- Resigned to your 'fate' – Something bad was bound to happen to me. That is how my life rolls.
- Whining – Why me? Why today?
- What am I going to dooooo?

To be honest, as I was writing, I laughed so hard at the cream cheese up the nose thing that I snorted *and* had tears in my eyes! It took quite a few minutes to get back mentally into writing. Then it occurred to me. A decade ago, I would have been that person. So, why did I laugh so hard? Because in that moment, mentally, I was the one in the car living the cream cheese incident and after the initial shock, laughing is *exactly* what I would have done. I am wowed by how far I've come in 10 years. Good news, that means you can too (and it doesn't have to take 10 years because you don't have to figure it out as you go like I did). Let's play this out some more.

In your drive time, you have further opportunity to choose how you will think about this situation. Even if you started out not so great, you still have the power to turn it around (silver lining). You could turn off the radio or audio book and think about why you reacted as you did. Instead of replaying the situation to further the anger or whining, let your thoughts run scenarios looking for clues. You are now in a fact-finding mode. A lot of insight happens when we get into a quiet place. The problem is, most people do not let quiet happen. They don't want to be left alone with their thoughts so they stay distracted with activities and devices all waking hours. For my note takers, make a note to look up mindfulness and intro-spection. Science is full of the positive impact they have on your current *and* future body and brain health, not to mention quality of life.

Again, there are endless possibilities of how this can turn out, but the truth is, from here, it's going to go mostly good or mostly bad. (That is not to say that there are not days when it comes at you, wave after wave of lemons. One hasn't hit the ground from bouncing off of you before the next two or three are landing. In these cases, you roll with it. You handle it *the exact same way* as a single assault. Remember, each lemon is an opportunity to choose. If you make a bad choice, guess what, you are in the driver's seat. Turn that right around with the very next thought, action, or word.) Here are the two basic scenarios to finish out this story to see how impactful what you think on is.

The hell option: Whether your radio or book was playing or not, you gnawed on those 'why me', 'why'd I even try this morning', 'bad things always happen to me', thoughts like a hungry dog goes at a bone. You can hear your heart pounding in your ears, your palms are sweaty, you're frustrated, and your chest feels constricted. Gone is the moment of the refreshing inhale/exhale. Your thoughts are jumbled, your pants are a mess, and to top it off, you're hungry and with every growl of your stomach, it just spins the recording again. As you walk down the hallway someone mentions the spot on your pants and like a dam that gave way, you spilled the whole story, arms flailing, voice raising, and tears welling in your angry and hurt eyes. Even if someone is empathic toward you, there is now tension in the hallway and people sort of slink away, and you feel even lower and probably embarrassed or maybe even angry that they didn't show much care for your horrible plight. This day, unless you make an adjustment to your thoughts (and you can at any time), is gonna suck. Plan on it.

The light at the end of the tunnel option: If you stopped the negative record and didn't let it play every time it tried to turn back on, you will find that your heart rate stays normal, you aren't sweaty or frantic, and, you'll most likely have a good day. Someone mentions the mark on your pants and you grin and come back with a fun, "I had a fight with a cream cheese bagel this morning", now pointing at your pants, "you can see who won!" concluding with a lighthearted chuckle. That will probably make them chuckle and maybe even share a personal antidote along the same lines. The atmosphere stays light and you continue to move, maybe even float through your day because you took a higher road, made a tough choice to stifle the 'I hate life because life hates me' thoughts that once dominated your mental space. *Stop is a powerful word.*

So, how did you do that? When the 'why me' or whatever familiar record started to play, you said stop. Whether you said stop mentally or verbally, you pushed the button that hushed the mental barrage and chose to see the situation in a different light. Depending on how deeply engrained the thoughts are, you may have to do it again. However, the more you do it, the more the old/bad fades away and is replaced with the new/good. It becomes easier. Do you remember when I told you that this will take guts? This is one of those times. It is not easy to go up against a brain poised to press play on the 'life sucks for me' button. But not this time. No more. I have said both out loud and, in my head, "no", "stop", and "that's enough" to stop the spinning. Whatever works for you, just hush it for a second so that you can record a different thought and start turning the situation.

That is step one, to stop the spinning, the downward spiral by not letting preprogramed negatives hold your mind hostage. Ok, now what? You can't just walk around with a blank mind all day. What do you fill it with? Let's find out!

Questions and Action Steps
Chapter Three

- Let's do an exercise to experience how powerful a thought is. You may need a timer if you easily get lost in thoughts.

1. For 60 seconds think about the worst part of your day or week. Now write down 1-5 words to describe how you currently feel and any bodily reactions that you had.

2. Next, for 60 seconds think about anything good rather things that happened to you or just good thoughts. How did your body change in that time? Did your blood pressure go back down? Did the hairs go from standing up to

> normal? Did you go from wanting to cry
> or crawl under the cushions to wanting
> to laugh or at least feeling less
> tumultuous inside?

That was a controlled example. Imagine doing this regularly in real life *as your day is going,* replacing negative thoughts with good ones. Take some time to imagine yourself adjusting your thoughts to increase your chances of a better emotional and mental outcome. Mental practice for the real thing is just like throwing the baseball in practice for the game. Even when you aren't battling an ugly thought or visual, you can still practice thinking of good or pleasant things. You can do this while showering, unloading the dishwasher, taking out the trash, any time.

- Are scenarios coming into mind where this can be effective? Are you starting to see how this is worth the mind retraining?

- There is a ton of material easily and freely available on positive thinking. You don't have to do it now, but put it on your calendar in the next few days to spend at least 30 minutes on this, especially something that is scientifically based. For whatever reason, we tend to believe, therefore act on, things that are proven.

- Start a discussion about this on the Discussion Group. Feedback is good and talking things through can widen your perspective. This is a tool for you. Use it.

Chapter 4
Changing Direction

Diving back in, keep in mind the more that you practice all of this, the quicker you get back to a healthy mindset and perspective. You'll also find that you can handle more without reaction, and eventually not even fall into the mind struggle trap. In any case, I am going to arm you to fully turn this thing into lemonade!

So, here you are, the survivor of a lemon attack. You have muted the 'poor me' recording and some-times, that is plenty enough to stop a potential spiral and continue on with your day. Sometimes, the thoughts or mental replays keep coming so you need to replace the negative mental chatter with some-thing positive. This gives less foothold to the old thoughts and helps to reprogram new ones. Imagine that you are in a situation and have said "no" to the negative thoughts. Assuming it's a doozie, and you cannot keep on as normal, what are you going to think on, right now, to start this spin in a positive direction?

For starters, you can never go wrong with things that are good, kind, honorable, and so forth. Find *any*thing that fits along those lines. And I mean *any*thing. It can be as simple as how delicious your coffee is, that your report was done on time, that you have clean water, that you are breathing fresh air. You think I am joking? No. There have been times when the bombarding thoughts got rough and I would get the spinning to stop and then think on the simplest things that were good just to hold steady as the momentum of the negative died down and the positive revved up. In those times, even thinking on those simple good things, in no time I could actually *feel* myself coming up.

Allow me to pause for a moment and remind you that I know that I don't know what you are going through right now. So, if I use a word, phrase or scenario that you cannot identify with, please accept the point and apply it accordingly. For example, if a storm has come through and you are three days without power and I suggest that you can be thankful for indoor heating/air conditioning, don't allow that to pull you down, use it to stir you up to find something that you can be thankful for. I'm telling you, there *always* is. (Look at Viktor Frankl and what he was able to do with the rest of his life and how many hundreds of thousands of lives are touched by his work to this day.)

I want to take this a step further and say that I understand that this may get deep at times, but you need to know how serious this is, as well as how powerful these truths are. You *can* change your life. Keep doing the work, taking the steps, making it happen. Revisit your notebook to see your progress. If you've been doing the work all this time, it's there.

To stop the spinning means to stop the chatter or visuals bombarding and sucking the very life from you. You can jump right in to good thoughts or things you may be grateful for, or if that is too tough, start with what you know right now to be a good truth, *no matter how small it is*. Just like a pepper seed, it may be tiny, but it is powerful! (Crazy kinds of hot in the case of some peppers!)

Ok, so what do we know to be (good) true, right

now? Is the sun shining? Great, you can get vitamin D. Is it raining? Great, the air is getting cleaned and the earth watered. Start as simply as you have to, but fill the gap to maintain the 'stop' and start the turn around. And let me say this. Even if all you have to start with is the fact that you are still breathing, that *is* something. That means that you have a chance, an opportunity. Once it's over, then what? Don't you want to know what happens if you don't quit?

Years ago, I heard a young man say, "What's worse than your story ending when you still have blank pages?" Let that sink in.

When you first start challenging the thoughts or visuals, or if it is a heavy mental bombardment, it's best to speak out loud (or under your breath if people are around) because you cannot run thoughts *and* speak at the same time, so speaking overrides the thoughts. Remember, you are retraining the way that you have thought for years. Just like you wobbled the first time you rode a bicycle, you may need to make some extra effort to get ahold of this new way of doing things. This is ok. I commend you for coming this far! What are some simple things that you can quickly go to, to change the mental chatter or ugly picture?

- I got to have a hot shower today.
- These old buildings (that I pass by every day) have some remarkable detail!
- I am glad I got to spend time with my friend today.
- Cell phones are a real help in my busy day!
- I love how excited my dog is to see me when I get home.
- That newly mowed grass smells good.

Yeah, *so* not kidding when I say *any*thing that is good or pleasant. It's better than feeling worthless, hurt, or increasingly angry... right?

You may find that, if possible, moving your body is helpful during these times as well. Even something as simple as standing can help. There's something about not sitting or lying down that helps you feel more in control of what's going on inside. Just give it a try and see what you think.

Moving on to the next level, you can take your thoughts and words higher and deeper. Remember, you have control over what you say and that too is very powerful. If the situation warrants, it would be great to reverse the thoughts with something positive. "No! (to the thought) I am actually *very* smart", "The truth is that I *am* valuable and worth the air I breathe", and so forth. This is an excellent way to *not only stop the record, but replace it quickly*. This is *re*training your mind so it may take a few times, but you'll feel a hint of confidence fire up inside of you each time you do it. It's great! And don't be concerned if you are angry or crying when you say those things. Speak to the thoughts anyway; through gritted teeth or breathless tears, speak it out. Stand up to those thoughts! Remember, emotions are fleeting and are *not* 'the' indicator of truth. Your truth is in your perspective, which is made up mostly by your mindset, and you are right in the middle of adjusting that. So, let your body have its trained reaction. Soon enough it too will line up with the newly built truth of your life.

Another way to help with the mental chatter is to turn on something worth listening to. (We will go further into what you watch and listen to in the next chapter.) When I was the one laid off as the economy started its downturn, the temptation was strong to 'why me' the scenario. A thought would flit in about this person who barely even did any work or that person who skated by on the least they could get away with, yet I was the one let go. I tried everything that I knew to do at that point and it would stop the thoughts for about 2.5 seconds. Geesh! I was already struggling and realizing that the slippery slope of self-pity was getting mighty close. Since I was driving, at the next stop light I grabbed my phone and turned on a motivational speech. I could not tell you what it was about, but I knew that if my mind had to focus on what was being said that it couldn't be talking back to me and telling me how rejected I was. I also knew that even though I wasn't fully paying attention to it, that I was getting quality input, stuff that would build me up, not push me down the pity party slide.

Take The Next Right Step

This book contains a buffet of ideas. Use what you have available to you to make it through the moment. And sometimes, that is all you can do is get through that moment. I saw this in an author unknown meme: "Sometimes the smallest step in the right direction ends up being the biggest step of your life". I agree wholeheartedly! Thinking back to some of the hardest times in my life, instead of participating in the pity party or anger fest, my inner voice would remind me, "just do what you know to do". Some-times that was just wash the dishes and listen to the birds outside. Sometimes that was go for a walk and think about better days ahead. Sometimes it was, it's late, go to bed. You get the idea. My sister says, "Do the next right thing". I like that rendition best because it can also mean, *not* sending the scathing text or email, *not* picking up the bottle of wine, and so-forth. Sometimes you may have a perceived 'back-slide'. You smoke another cigarette, eat the whole container of ice cream, or swipe the credit card again. Consider this: if you made it through what could have been a tougher moment, say, the shopping kept you from saying something you would regret later like quitting your job, smoking kept you from cutting yourself, eating the ice cream gave you time to pause which kept you from going back into the abusive scenario, then that counts as making a next right step. This is not an exact science, so use common sense. See this not as permission to make excuses, but to be human. Be kind to yourself and realize that as you continue to grow, you will not need those fall backs.

The Game Changer

Earlier it was brought up that talking to the negative thoughts and replacing them with positive while being your own mental and verbal cheerleader are good and powerful actions and should be a lifelong habit. I have learned to congratulate myself when I make a hard choice in the right direction and it feels like someone lit a candle inside of me. It doesn't warm you all up or shed a huge light on anything, but it makes a difference in the right direction instead of tearing yourself down and becoming darker, sadder, and even more defeated than before. With that said, are you ready for a bonus concept?

Go with me on this. Once you grasp the power of what I'm about to say, no matter how weird you feel doing it, the first time you experience its power, you will wield it like a sword, instigating change faster and with longer lasting results! You *really* want to stop the spinning and internal crazy talk? Sing. Yes, sing. Even when you don't feel like it. (Feel free to look up the science that backs this, but I am telling you experientially, it works, even through tears!) Make up the words if you have to. You are taking back what is yours, telling your mind that your will, your choice, has more authority than mental visuals or thoughts wanting to dominate you. You decide!

Over the years, I have put together a playlist of 'I got this' songs for varying scenarios. Two of my favorites are Michael Bublé's rendition of *Feeling Good* and *Nobody's Watching* by Hollywood

Undead. I have listened to and sung along with those songs many times when things were rough and the thoughts wanted to take me down; meaning, I wasn't actually 'feeling good' and I sure didn't feel like 'singing like nobody's watching', but when I did it anyway, **it was nothing short of miraculous!** It is the ultimate emotional pain relief and when you aren't in pain, you have clearer headspace. It won't fix the immediate problem. I mean, the dog is dead. The fire left nothing but piles of charred lumber and ash where the house once stood. When you are singing (even with tears rolling down your face) it doesn't take long and the spinning slows down and you can grab ahold of your thoughts and turn them around again. Hope rises up and then, there it is, the silver lining. Answers start to come. They trickle in or sometimes they just plop right in front of you. This is a very quick way out of what could become a really bad situation. Who cares what people, or even your own mind thinks about it? Sing anyway. The idea is to get out of pain and move forward, right? So, do what you've got to do to make that happen as fast as possible!

In case it needs to be said, the words in the songs need to be uplifting. I have heard bouncy songs that encourage suicide. So *pay attention to the words.* As an example, my favorite line in *Nobody's Watching* is "It's times like this, I feel I'm on the pavement. It's like my heart's so numb. Then I grab that book and turn the pages, to see how far I've come." (That's usually the part where I start to dance or bounce if I am driving!) Make sure that the words are healthy ones.

Putting It All Together

Ok, let's keep the train moving and sum this up. What's the main idea here? *As soon as* you recognize that you are thinking on the wrong stuff, stop and reverse it. I know that it sounds cooky, but as previously pointed out, the other way wasn't working, so let's give this a go. Who cares what your pride thinks? Chunk that mess and get on board with mind renewal. Pride (different from self-respect) will keep you tethered to the past and to hurtful things and it doesn't care that you are disintegrating. Tell it to leave and put on a new way of doing things; something that will actually garner results! Continuing to roll negative thoughts over in your mind that make your insides feel like squirrels are tearing through you will only make it worse. There is no escaping that pain when you think on it, and think on it, and see it over and over in your mind. *Stop the craziness!* Use any of these ideas and as you continue, prepare to be amazed at how the pain dissipates. (Remember the July 4 story and how changed I was in just two laps around the block after hours of misery?) It may be only for a moment, but we just need relief that one moment. We will take on the next moment at that time. This builds and soon you won't even recognize the situation and will be in full amazement on how well you came out on the other side. You'll wanna hug me. And I'm cool with that.

Before we move into the questions, I'd like to slow the pace and chat with you for a moment. You have already encountered some life altering ideas. Just applying what you have learned thus far, you have adjusted your trajectory. Congratulations! As we progress, please keep a few things in mind:

- As I stated earlier, there's no judgement. You are reading this book and doing the best that you know to do where you are right now. Perfection doesn't work. Let go of the idea of getting it perfect every day and all of the time. Now, that doesn't give you permission to not try, but it *does* give you permission to be human. When the football player tumbles while the ball is still in play, he doesn't need to take his time getting back up, dust his uniform, and straighten his jersey before he takes off again. No. He's gotta get up as fast as possible and get back in the game. *That is you.* Who cares that you ate another piece of pie or cried a bit past the healthy stage (we'll get to that in another chapter). Just recognize it and get back in the game.

- You aren't what you *were*, you're who you *are*. At this moment you are changing into something better and more awesome. You are taking ownership of your life and its outcome and becoming stronger, more courageous and confident as you do. See *that* person each day. It may take practice, but please, see him/her. That is who you are. Grow into *that* person. Don't be held back by yesterday. The best way to not be who you were is what you are doing right now: shaking free of the past. You're doing great!

- I've made multiple mentions that this will take guts, courage, strength. You are probably starting to see that I wasn't making that up. This isn't easy, but when is something worthwhile easy? However, I'd like to encourage you that it will get easy-*er*. Whenever you do something new for the first time it can be a challenge. *Just because this isn't tangible doesn't make it any different.* You didn't become a great cook, writer, plumber, painter, teacher, parent, athlete, etc overnight. No, you went over the basics until you had a good handle on them and then added to it. That is all that we are doing here. You may sweat or cry or swear or pace or run or take a zillion showers or whatever you have to do to make it through that moment. Remember, it is just a moment, in a sea of moments, and your choice, *right then*, to take the higher, harder road is what steers you into a better direction. *These are choices you will never regret.* Doing the better thing *will* pay off. Granted, it may not be as instantaneous as we would like, but it comes easier. I remember when heartbreak would derail me for weeks. The last one derailed me for about an hour (and that story is a real head shaker). I am not cold and heartless. I just know how to step through it better than I did 10 years, 5, years, even *a* year ago. And maybe one day it will be even less time than that (or maybe my days of heartbreak are over? lol).

Thank you for allowing me to chat with you. Now that we have a good handle on managing thoughts, let's talk about a few more perspective shifts as well as guarding your heart and mind to keep the momentum. Ready? Let's do it!

Questions and Action Steps
Chapter Four

- What are some go to phrases or general positive thoughts that you can keep in your back pocket when it gets mentally rough? What truths are you going to replace those recordings with the next time they pop up? Just thinking on those and/or writing them down, do you feel lighter, freer, more hopeful? Powerful, isn't it???

- I brought up what the young man said years ago: "What's worse than your story ending when you still have blank pages?" I know that we took a few moments to let that sink in. Now I'm asking you to write down how that applies to you. What does that mean to you right now? And what do some of your pages look like on the other side of this? or 3 months from now or 6... how about 10 years from now? Will that person be thanking you for remaining in the game? (This would be a great share in the Discussion Group. It could be a real encourager or make us think sort of topic.)

- Find a song or two that you can have at the ready should you need to "sing like nobody's watching". (You can get a head start by visiting the resources for this book section at MsJoysPlace.com)

Chapter 5
Redirect Your Life by Being Your Own Gatekeeper

You're doing it! Now that you are seeing and experiencing how powerful mindset is, are you feeling more confident? More hopeful that you really *can* direct your todays and tomorrows? Keep working on it. This is gonna be SO GREAT!

Teacher and author Sue Hadfield said, "It takes courage to examine your life and to decide that there are things you would like to change, and it takes even more courage to do something about it." I am so proud of you for making it this far and continuing this path!!

You are working diligently to watch for the decision point, not let your thoughts dominate you, change your mental landscape, speak kindly to yourself, possibly adding a happy tune, and choosing to see the path out; in short you are taking the higher and truthfully, harder, road. How can you maximize this effort and not slip backward into old patterns? You need a few more perspective adjustments as well as guard your heart and mind. Guarding the heart and mind require many of the same things and each can benefit from the effort of protecting the other so going forward, when one is being spoken about, apply it to the other as well. Let's start with two perspective shifts.

#1 It's Not Just You

You are not the only one that this has happened to. I know that sounds harsh and if you are currently hurting, maybe that sounds all out cruel. I promise that I do not intend to hurt you. Let's look at this from a different angle and in doing so, it will greatly help the healing and growing process.

Knowing that you aren't the only one that this has happened to sets you free from the debilitating lie that no one understands what you are going through. Don't go there. *This isolation is dangerous and increases the speed of the downward spiral.* "But Joy, my situation is different". I promise you, the exact details and order in which they happened may be different, but in all the time that humans have lived on this earth, someone somewhere, and more likely many people everywhere have experienced what you have. You aren't the only one that was molested, falsely accused, stolen from, humiliated, discarded/rejected, lost their job, laughed at, saw someone murdered, used, buried a family member, friend, pet, and so on. You aren't the only one that has a medical diagnosis, lives in pain, has been treated unjustly, parents got divorced, didn't get what you want... as you can see, I could go on and on.

Consider this. Think of the thousands and thousands of love songs out there. *Most* of them are about heartbreak. Now, 1) why would an artist make one song for just one person in all the world? and 2) Why are these songs so popular? Because most people can identify with them. Or look at this. Why are there so many support groups if you are the only one who has dealt with divorce, grief, substance abuse, overeating, etc? Because so many people can identify with it. This same thinking is applied to TV shows and movies. Why can we identify with the main character? I promise, you are not the only person in that theater that 'gets' him/her. We can all feel their pain in some way. Hopefully by now you realize that your scenario doesn't make you unique. That's good because you don't have to go it alone. Remember, someone has walked this road before you. Seek out a group, counselor, book, podcast, video, etc on the subject. Knowledge is power. It'll move you through the pain and situation faster on a paved road than trudging through an unknown jungle of 'how'?

#2 Grieving vs Pity Party

Hurting over your loss (grief) is natural and feeling sorry for yourself over the loss is part of it and has a place in healing *to a point*. The bottom line is that tears and anger and 'this sucks' are *real*. Don't try to choke it back. It is ok to express pain. That is natural. So cry. Punch the punching bag, pillow, or the air. Yell, fume, ball your fists, curl up, go for a run or walk, whatever. Feel the feeling; let your body express the ouch. *The key is to not let it take over you.* At some point, the bag of cookies is gone, the tissues have been used up, you've punched the air so much you started a dust storm, and so on. You're done. It's expressed. Now stop.

Should you take this to pity party level, you have just set yourself up to swim around in the muck and if you allow others to party with you, you've just empowered the situation to hold your mind, emotions and ultimately your life captive. You will stay stuck, right there as things grow more and more grim and painful, as they further fall apart, and you like yourself less and less. Oh, there is the temporary relief of people partying with you (cheering you up, buying you food, handing you tissues, etc) but at some point, it will get old for them too; then what? The parent is still dead, the car is still repossessed, you still need to find a job. But look at you. What happened here? You got on the slide and went right back down down down to where the circumstances put you and possibly worse. You're there on your back in a pool of lemon juice. The tears have dried up, and life continued on all around you and there you are lemon juice wrinkly and nothing to show for your days and nights, but feeling worse about yourself than when the lemon pelting began.

Your take away: cry, yell, run, stand in the rain, beat the air, whatever, until you are spent and then it is time to take charge of things again. Depending on the depth, this expression step can last a few hours and it is ok if emotions arise again later. For example, my very dear friend died and I cried upon hearing the expected news (she had cancer). I made it the next few days fairly normal and then the funeral came and I cried again, this time, it starting to hit me. Driving away, I determined as I passed the big monument at the cemetery exit that going forward, I would remember the good times we had and know that I will see her again and choose to smile and allow those things to fill my heart and mind. But the day came, a few days after the funeral that I text her and it wasn't until after I pressed 'send' that I realized, she will not be responding to that text. I will never see her name come up on my notifications list ever again. That hit me *hard*. Crying again, I text that part her too, told her I loved her and that I looked forward to seeing her again someday and then deleted all of our messages and her contact. I know me; I will go back and reread those messages over and over again, pulling the band aid off and re-opening the wound and never fully heal. So for me, it needed to be deleted. I let myself be in that moment, fulling expressing the sense of loss that came with the no more texts realization.

About 20 minutes later, tears having subsided, I knew it was expressed and it's time to step along. As you can see, I let myself experience each time a new level of realization hit me, but I didn't *stay* in each beyond its time. Today I can think fondly of her with a smile on my face and warmth in my heart and not hurting because my beloved friend is gone. And to be fair, her husband and daughters had their own healing journey because they knew her in a different way than I did. Again, this book is not an end all. I am not blowing off grief (and we can grieve all sorts of things, even a job to retirement). I am giving you the steps and then you apply them, as often as needed, to move through this and any other situation while remaining softhearted, kind, generous, and loving.

So yes, emotions coming up as you go through the healing process is natural and part of moving through it. Just make sure you are doing that; moving through it. It is easy to get stuck in pause because we think that that will somehow delay the painful parts. No, the day will come and further realizations of the loss impact on your life comes to light. (Whatever that loss or life altering event is.) Continue to use what you have learned so when that well-meaning (or not) friend comes along, "Giiiiirl, I can *not* believe that they fired you!", you can find a way to put up your hand and say, "It's ok, I get to try my hand at something new" or whatever you have in your mind that is your (good) truth about the situation. For me, when I would get a hug with "I'm so sorry for your loss", I was able to receive the hug knowing that (at least in the case of losing my friend), people meant well, and I was able to honestly say, "Thank you. I am looking forward to seeing her again" and then smile. It was a tiny smile in the first few weeks, but today, years later, my heart beams at the idea!

Please understand that I am *fully aware* of how real loss, rejection, unfairness and the like feels. I do not expect you to be a hard and mean person with tons of protective walls up. I tried those. They don't work. They suffocate and kill you slowly. Those who know me today know that I am a soft, kind hearted person. How is that possible? Doing what I am laying out here for you to do. What we are doing, is giving the body and mind an opportunity to express the emotion and then get back to balance and not stay stuck with the pendulum swung way in one direction. Just like you may express happiness in a situation as a laugh or dancing, you cannot do that night and day. Laying around in a sad state or being an anger bomb isn't realistic nor healthy. Balance. Express the emotion healthfully in the moment, collect yourself, and step forward. Rinse and repeat. I'm here to tell you, it gets easier. Not because you are hardened, but because you have experienced that this process works. It is like the valve letting the pressure out and then balance can come back in.

Garbage In, Garbage Out

Now let's discuss guarding your heart and mind. We have heard the phrase 'you are what you eat'. Well, what you watch and listen to becomes a part of who you are as well. If you don't believe me, here's a little test that you can do. When you are happy and want to dance around, watch 10 minutes of the news. How do you feel now? No so great. And if you feed on the bad, negative, ugly, day in and out, what is training your thoughts? Where are they being directed? Surely by now, you know that I am not suggesting that you put your head in the sand, but do you have to gorge on that stuff?

What are you feeding on? (Think about the wolf story. Now think about your social media "feeds".) Who are you hanging around, texting, talking with on the phone? You need to take control of the input and be your own gatekeeper. You may need to remove yourself from some social groups, social media feeds, turn off the television, your phone, etc while you get your feet under you. If you do spend time on social media, make sure that it is stuff that builds you up, makes you laugh, enhances your life, and brings you closer to your goals.

As it is possible, surround yourself with people

that support this effort. Definitely spend time reading, watching, and listening to things that encourage
your more healthful behavior, but avoid those that
make you feel yuck; whatever that is for you. If you
want a place to start to set a new pattern, do a search
on 'positive mental attitude'. That may be what you
have to run to as your 'fix' to stop the craziness for
the moment. You want something to watch, listen to
or look at, but the other stuff is just dragging you
down? Run to a better alternative. Take charge of
your mind and heart. Guard it *because your life
really does depend on it.*

Soar Higher

Another way to guard your mind and heart is to stay
above the fray. This is a phrase that came up inside
of me many years ago when I was in the middle of
drama drama drama. I didn't want to be 'that person'
anymore, the one that was impacted by the he
said/she said. I didn't want it to touch me. I was
already hurting, betrayed, and humiliated. I just
wanted away from it all! By then I had stopped the
negative mental chatter and kept replacing the
thoughts with good truths and the way that I wanted
to be, but kept getting sucked back in by the texts

and conversations/gossip that was only hurting me more. That's when I heard it: "stay above the fray". In that moment, I remembered that the eagle flies *above* the storm clouds and is having the time of its life while those of us below the clouds are scampering for cover as the lightning strikes and thunder booms. Once you have decided that you've had enough, it is fairly easy to take yourself outside of the circle of destruction and above the fray away from the mess. Simply remove yourself from the physical ties (texts, posts, phone calls) and then mentally deciding the soar above it all. Don't participate. If someone cornered me pushing to discuss it, I simply said no thank you and walked away *without apology*. That is a key. You can respectfully hold your ground by saying "I do not want to discuss this" and if they cannot honor your request, leave. It really is that simple, and yes you can do it and no it is not rude. They were the rude ones by not honoring your request to drop the subject. I was in so much emotional pain and they weren't helping; they just wanted to be a part of the drama. Not me. I walked off stage and didn't look back! By then, I didn't care who was mad at me. They were only mad because they couldn't get the juicy inside gossip. Is that really a friend? Is that really love? That is a whole other subject, but you know what I mean and you know I am telling you the truth. It is *your* heart, guard it.

What does staying above the fray look like? When my mind wanted to repeat what I had read or the things that I had heard or if my insides started to scream in agony, I would double blink to stop the thought (that was my personal cue) and immediately take my mind up higher. To get started I would imagine being the eagle flying past the storm clouds of the gossip and pain. Eventually I was able to elevate my thoughts up higher and didn't need the cue or visuals. You just have to give it a try and you will see what I mean. Stay above the fray. Don't get embroiled in the mess. You're better than that.

This chapter gave a hand*ful* of guards to set up/perspectives to adjust. You may want to take some time to really digest them. The chapter questions will help. Remember that a good attitude and disposition go a long way in healing and restoration. There is a ton of science to back that up. Now let's look at some solid ways to employ this idea so that you can become stronger.

Questions and Action Steps
Chapter Five

- What are you thinking on? What are you watching, listening to? What are you letting into your heart/mind that could be derailing your efforts?

- Do you need to remove things/people/shows, etc from your environment? If so, what/whom and how and when will you be doing this?

- What are you going to replace some of the negative input with?

- Share your ideas and commitments with the Discussion Group. We can help you stay on track and you can help others keep their course as well. The resources on my website can be useful as well.

Chapter 6
Maintaining and Continuing to Grow

U p to this point you have been learning to survive, float not sink, put one foot in front of the other, and the spinning has stopped. If you haven't been able to put words to what you are feeling, that's called hope. That glimmer that we talked about early in the book; that little fire inside of you realizing that this really could be something life changing. Now it's time to take it up a notch and maintain the ground that you have worked so diligently to take. Are you ready to sink your teeth in and get down to business? Let's do this!

Your attitude is a door that swings whichever way you choose. The last chapter discussed guarding your heart and mind by keeping the negative out (or at least reducing it) and seeking out things that build you up and take you to a healthier place. What you think on, discuss, and engage in makes up your attitude. A rotten attitude brings absolutely no peace or resolution in your life. It just gums it up and keeps your worries and troubles in place like ever drying cement. With that in mind, it's my strong belief and repeated experience that a positive attitude will lose you from those bonds and move you over the mountain, around the corner, through the darkness to a happier place and will help you to maintain your progress so that you can go up even higher!

When you want to have a healthier body, you have to put quality food in it, and to have a healthier attitude or mindset, you have to employ quality character traits and actions. Guarding your heart and mind is step one, no doubt, but that just keeps things from getting worse. Ingesting information about growing as a person or things that make you happy solidifies a stronger and better mental space thereby mindset thus perspective then actions and finally life as you experience it.

Let's go deeper to 'healthy up' the attitude, by choosing not to quit, learning about the power of forgiveness, leaving vengeance alone, why comparison is harmful, and the benefits of gratitude, boundaries, hope, purpose, celebration, and acceptance.

These are not the only healthful traits we can adjust to, but they are great starting points. I am going to touch on each subject giving a general overview and if you would like to learn more about any of these topics there are many resources readily available for you to dig in to!

After reading that list you may be moaning wondering if Joy is going to cue up Kum-ba-ya. Remember the 3 month down the road version of you that we discussed previously? They want to be here, now. *This* is how they get here. Germany Kent said "Never underestimate the power you have to take your life in a new direction." C'mon, let's do this!

Don't Quit

Here is where I say don't quit. You knew it was coming! LOL! Below are just a handful of quotes about not quitting. Stick at least one of these, or another that you like, in your mental pocket (better yet, write it down and keep it with you) and pull it out as often as needed. Let's be honest, this can get wearying, especially when you are first doused in lemon juice. And if for some reason it drags on a bit or there is severe pain, you can grow tired. What we are doing takes courage; I know. And I also know that you have it in you!

Keep these in mind:

- Difficulty is the one excuse that history never accepts. – Edward R. Murrow
- Prove them wrong.
- A diamond is just a piece of charcoal that handled stress exceptionally well.
- The person that you are a year from now will thank you for not quitting.
- You can either throw in the towel, or use it to wipe the sweat off your face.
- At any given moment, you have the power to say this is not how the story is going to end.
- I didn't come this far to only come this far.
- Pain is temporary. If I quit, however, it lasts forever. – Lance Armstrong

Forgiveness Is For You

Forgiveness is for you, not them. It releases you from the hurt and entanglement, allowing you to be free to move about life unhindered. Have you ever had someone come to you weeks, months, or years later and tell you about that thing that you said or did and how it hurt them and you stand there, doe-eyed like "huh"? All this time they were in pain over it and you don't even *remember* doing/saying it! Even if someone intentionally hurt you, they still get to move on with life. So why are you going to allow that person's actions toward you keep *you* in the mud? Forgiving them is the key that unwraps the chains from your heart, mind, and life. Forget about if they 'deserve' it or not. Listen to me, not forgiving them doesn't hurt them. *Not one bit.* But it could eventually kill *you*. They aren't worth it.

Leave Vengeance Alone

Vengeance isn't our business. I am not old, but I have lived long enough to see that what goes around, does come back around (good and bad). Leave it alone. Stay above the fray. Hands off. It'll happen. They will get theirs. You keep your nose on your own face, focus on healthy and right, clean up your life and leave them to theirs. You'll see. I read somewhere years ago 'The best revenge is a life well lived'. Shake the dust off and move on. Use the tools in this book to help you.

Comparison

To finish my partial quote, "keep your nose on your own face and run your own race". The comparison trap will hold you hostage eating away at your self esteem and causing you to always scramble to feel good enough. Do yourself a favor and only compare you to you. How? Look at where you were X time ago and where you are now. Have you changed for the better? Great! Not so much, then do something about it. Make each version of you a better version. Put the clay back on that spinny thing and mold your life to be what you want. Let others handle their business and you handle yours.

The Power Of Being Grateful

Gratitude, being grateful or thankful, these are words and phrases we have heard. There's a reason. They're powerful! Author Neale Donald Walsch said, "The struggle ends when the gratitude begins". There's truth here. Taking the time to be and express gratitude and thankfulness is your path to freedom and more goodness in your life. It changes your view on everything and then, as if by magic, opportunities, options, and doors seem to appear. Things that you didn't see before are right in front of you. But wait there's more! You aren't miserable in the process! Whhaaaaat? Yep. When you decide to find the good in the situation or that thing you can be thankful for, somehow your insides start to loosen up, the stress dissipates and light shines on the situation. Give it a try. Thinking of even one thing to be grateful for begins to shift your mind from grumble, moan, complain, and bleck to possibility, hope, lightheartedness and so on. *It's like a magnet, bringing more things to be grateful for the more you employ it.*

Boundaries Keep You Safe

My friend Melissa was learning about the power of boundaries and sharing a recent success with me saying, "Being healthy is not letting their tornado of emotions in my yard." Exactly! Boundaries are not just to keep the bad out, but the good in. They aren't supposed to be walls, but a permeable state where you let stuff in and out. Just like you would check the peephole before opening your front door, you check your insides to make sure that your boundaries aren't being overrun. An example is making the quality decision to not allow yourself to be spoken to in an unkind manner. A boundary would be, 'I don't want to be spoken to like that so please don't'. And if a person cannot honor that request, then they do not get the benefit of your presence as you walk away. There doesn't have to be an attitude. Just a quiet expectation that the neat little fence you put up would be respected. There is freedom in boundaries and has the added benefit of increasing your confidence and overall outlook on things.

Hope Is Not Wishful Thinking

Hope is a confident expectation of something good. Just saying that word 'hope' puts a lightness in the air. Hope keeps the fire inside burning while you take the next step. It is a powerful force to keep you in the game.

Purpose

Having a purpose is what gets you willingly out of bed in the morning. So, why are you here? What would make you jump out of bed in the morning? When you are dragging through your days and nights with no purpose there doesn't feel like there's much worth continuing for. Well, I believe that you are breathing for a reason, so please use resources available to you to find what that is and get on it. Start building the life you want instead of letting it just happen to you. You are already on your way just by reading and applying the lessons of this book. Great job!

Celebrate!

"We celebrate every victory large or small" is something I have said for decades. Why not dance, rejoice, high five, grin real big, and enjoy something good that has happened or been accomplished? Whenever something went right or you accomplished something you'd set your mind to, go ahead and acknowledge it. Take 15 seconds and enjoy that moment and if appropriate share it with someone else and receive their congratulations, pat on the back, hand shake, or other form of celebrating with you. It's nice to be invited to a celebration, even the 15 second ones!

Acceptance Is A Real Eye Opener

Acceptance can be a tricky one to wrap your mind around so stay with me here. Acceptance isn't sucking it up and feeling helpless. It is acknowledging that something simply 'is' and not assigning an emotion to it so that you can evaluate where you are in relation to that issue. For example: I accept that there is a traffic light on every corner on my way to work. I accept that Bob and I don't see eye to eye on everything. I accept that it is raining. Let's get deeper. I accept that he died. I accept that the company is closing my department. I accept that the tree fell on the house. Accepting things as they are helps to put them in a realistic place so that you aren't crazy that it cannot be changed by you. It allows you to look at the scenario as a fact so that you can then choose your path toward or away from it. It frees you of the emotions holding you to that situation so that you can start a new journey, tread a new path. You may not like the idea of the unknown, but this situation has changed your life. Accepting it will untie you from this viewpoint and open up avenues you may never have known existed.

You have placed the scenario as a fact without emotion or judgement in front of you. Now perspective it. The truth is, the traffic light is needful in all of those spots even though I don't like the red ones. Like me, Bob has a free will and is allowed to think differently than I do even though I'd love for us to agree on everything, and we have been needing rain and I can still have my picnic. I just moved it inside! This applies to the deeper 'acceptances' too. Some of the most amazing stories start when there is a change or conflict (think of the best movies you have seen. When did it get start getting good? When change occurred). It has been 10 years since my family went on that camping trip. I didn't know that I could recover. Look at me now! It started with me accepting that my life would not look the same again.

Expansion: Continue To Grow

By now you should be seeing some progress and the pain is gone or at least easing up. If you are not seeing that, I will remind you to revisit your journal. If you haven't, you really need to. You need to see how far you have come; be amazed at how differently you'd answer the first questions. Seeing your progress is very helpful because it's proof that you are moving.

You and I have come far together and have arrived at the final part! Here we will discuss expansion, how you will continue to grow. There is so much personal growth 'fertilizer' out there that I cannot provide an exhaustive list, but I will equip you with some starting points in no specific order.

What catapults you to another level may just inch another person forward so test things out and keep at it. There is no excuse for you to not continue this momentum. Here I am, hand reached out toward you, asking you to step up further. The view is *uh-MAY-zing* up here. Come and see for yourself!

- MsJoysPlace.com was built with resources and the Discussion Group created for you!
- Support groups: Depending on what you are going through, there may be a support group out there such as Divorce Care, Alcoholics Anonymous, Grief Share, and more. You may not need something so direct. Maybe just a mommy group for stay-at-home moms or a couple's group in your local community or church. The idea of a support group isn't to drape yourselves over each other and moan and cry; it's for 'support', to know that you aren't the only one, to feel like if they can get through it so can I, to learn tips on how to do it better or faster or to get other resources. Don't let pride or fear keep you from stepping into a

support group. Worst case is you didn't like it. Ok, find another one. Do not go this alone. [I'm giving you *that* look, just sayin'.]

- Podcasts and videos: There is so much free stuff online, just do a search and listen or watch until you get to someone that you resonate with then go all in.

- Library: Your library has videos, CDs, books, online resources and if they do not offer what you need, you can usually do an interlibrary loan, for free or very minimal cost. Dive in. Swim in this stuff. Renew your mind to a new life and a new way!

- Counseling: Depending on your situation it may do some good to speak with someone to give you some perspective. Many employers have EAP (Employee Assistance Program) where they pay for a certain number of sessions and it is anonymous. It's also good sometimes to just talk to someone that doesn't know you so that you can speak freely.

- Move your body: Go for a walk, hike, swim, climb. Ride a bike, go to the gym or online and look up workouts. Start with a 10 minute one or pick a longer one and do what you can. There are 'how to dance' and dance workout videos online too. The idea is to move your body. Pick something you like or would like to try. If you don't like it, try something different tomorrow. Again, just move your body. It is so great for stress relief and clearing your mind!

- Sing-Laugh-Dance: Why not put on your favorite song and sing it at the top of your lungs while you hold the Sharpie as your microphone? Or dance like you don't care who sees you? And laugh. Laugh until your side hurts. Just start laughing. It feels dumb at first, but keep doing it, and before you know it, you are laughing for real and you may get so good at it that you snort! LOL!! Yes, I have done every one of these things.

- Volunteer: Give back. It doesn't have to be a huge thing, but going to your local animal shelter to play with the dogs means the world to them and to the overworked staff. Walk into a shelter and ask where they need help. Carry a plastic bag with you and pick up garbage along the hiking trail making a better environment for humans and animals alike. Get creative or just reach out as you see someone in need.

- Do or learn something new: Put some adventure into your life. This will change your point of view and open your mind. Try a new meal at the same restaurant, go to a different restaurant, take a different route home, read a book, do a different type of workout, hold your glass or spoon with the other hand, find some random video on a subject you don't know much about and indulge for 3-5 minutes. Just do something different or new. Shake things up. Get out of your comfort zone. Walk the opposite direction, cook instead of ordering out, little things. You don't have to do big things to change it up a bit. The idea is to get out of your rut and to see life that is all around you that you normally pass by or would never see had you not made that change. Groupon is a good starting point for ideas.

- Adventure idea: You can do this alone or with others. Grab a coin and decide if heads or tails is left and then the other will be right. Start walking, bike riding, or driving. When you get to a place that you can turn, flip. Have a predetermined idea of how many flips you will make before you stop. Once you stop, do/experience wherever you are. So, if you end up at a shopping center, go into one of the stores or restaurants. If you end up at a park, slide down the slide or swing on the swing. I'm not sure that you should get a tattoo if you land at the parlor unless you are feeling super adventurous, but you get the idea. Let me know how your adventure turns out! (I seriously would love to know.)
- Journal: Continue the practice you have begun. Adding in things that you are grateful for each day is especially helpful to keep the light turned on inside. Remember, the more you express

gratitude, the more you experience
things to be grateful for. Journaling helps
create victories because you can see
where you have been compared to who
you are now. It builds confidence
because you realize what you have made
it through. Those are your trophies for
not giving up!

This should get you started and there's even more that you will find as you step out. I am excited to hear what you chose to do and how it impacted you! We are nearly done, but our journey doesn't have to end here. Keep in touch. I want to celebrate your successes with you! As you have come to expect, there are some questions for you to answer and then we will meet up once more to find out what's next.

Questions and Action Steps
Chapter Six

- To overcome your situation and maintain your progress takes next level mind renewal by resetting habits and perspectives.

1. What is the first perspective shift that you are going to employ and why?

2. Which perspective shift are you hesitant to take on and why? Are you willing to use available resources to help you overcome this? If so, I encourage you to do it now while you have made the quality decision to do it and if not, please come back to this question in a week and give it another thought.

- What does the dialogue with you and 6-months-from-now-you look like? How is it different than the one you were having at the end of Chapter 1?

- What will you do to continue this momentum?

Chapter 7
Now What? Rinse and Repeat

You've done it! You made it through the book and you have tools in your belt. I don't know where you are on your path right now, how fast or slow you read the book, or what your mental presence was during it. What I do know is that you can go back through this as many times as you need to, always with your notebook, always looking for a fresh perspective, always employing a new way, always growing and becoming better. *It's measurable.* You live with you so you may not see it, but look at your journal. You'll see!

Coach John Wooden said , "Do not let what you cannot do interfere with what you can do." Don't get hung up on the specifics or what seems impossible right now. Remember, take the next step. Do the next right thing. Do what you *can*.

Now is a good time to reflect on where you have been and where you want to be as that directs where you will go. Ask yourself how you see your situation now. 'Who' are you now? What defines you now? If any of it has a negative feel, how can you change it? What perspective can you take to adjust the lens?

Remember, that you, *only you*, hold the key to your happiness. Turn it as needed until the door that you want opened is unlocked. Finally, please share your stories with me and please please *please* know how so very proud I am of you!!!! Gigantic hugs, high fives, and huge smiles.

Action Steps and Information

- If this book has helped you, would you please leave a review so that others can find it as well?
- I would be *thrilled* to hear your story! Please send it to me or better yet, share it with the Discussion Group so that we can all cheer.

- Lastly, I have more books in the works for you. If you would like to be notified when a book is available, please let me know.
- You can reach me at MsJoysPlace.com or hello@msjoysplace.com or on various social media outlets.

Have a wonderful day!! **You got this**!

Bibliography

Frankl, V. E. (2022). *Man's Search for Meaning 1st (first) edition Text Only*.

General Patton. (2022, September 28). *Quotes*. http://generalpat ton.com/quotes/

Hardy, B. P. (2015). *Slipstream Time Hacking: How to Cheat Time, Live More, And Enhance Happiness* (2nd ed.).

If life hands you a lemon, don't complain, but instead make lemonade to sell to those who are thirsty from complaining. (2020, June 16). Napoleon Hill Foundation. https://www. naphill.org/tftd/thought_for_the_day_06-16-20/

Kutless - What Faith Can Do (Official Music Video). (2010, February 13). [Video]. YouTube. https://www.youtube.com/ watch?v=u1JBSQMkQE0

Man's Search for Ultimate Meaning. (2000). Basic Books.

Motivational Quotes. (2016, October 11). Coach John Wooden. https://www.thewoodeneffect.com/motivational-quotes/

Moving Forward is a Choice. (2015, September 14). Ziglar Inc. https://www.ziglar.com/quotes/getting-knocked-down-in-life-is-a-given/

About the Author

Joy has always felt a strong calling to help others, leading her to volunteer in various capacities including mentoring, which she done for more than 20 years. During that time, she has helped people from all walks of life and ages face and overcome the darkest moments of their lives as well as those who have huge dreams that they were unable to achieve because of life's hard knocks. Joy has carried on her work as a mentor with great enthusiasm and love, creating strong bonds with many of them. As the years progressed Joy began to understand how much strength is needed to face the challenges with which life tests us, often finding us unprepared, and realizing how important it is to take small steps to solve any problem and achieve lasting results.

In addition to her work as a mentor, Joy has a love for writing and has trained those skills by ghostwriting and copy editing for over 20 years. Finally combining her two passions, Joy is now sharing her experiences in dealing with personal growth and overcoming the odds through her books that are designed as short reads that are easy to understand, and with the intention of removing the obstacle of the struggle of starting, which aids in continuing her readers' journey of growth.

She also offers a private discussion group for her readers to share, celebrate and encourage one another. Come join the community!

Join the Discussion!

MsJoysPlace.com
Resources, Articles,
Links, and More!

Other Social Media
@MsJoysPlace

email:
hello@msjoysplace.com

Use the QR Code for the Social Media of your choice or for the Discussion Group only, choose that QR code or go to
www.facebook.com/groups/msjoysplace